CAT PEOPLE

CAT PEOPLE

BILL HAYWARD

WITH AN INTRODUCTION BY
ROGERS E. M. WHITAKER, THE OLD CURMUDGEON

A DOLPHIN BOOK

DOUBLEDAY & COMPANY, INC., GARDEN CITY, NEW YORK

DESIGNED BY LAURENCE ALEXANDER

Introduction © 1978 by Rogers E. M. Whitaker

Portions of this book have appeared in the March 1978 issue of *Ladies' Home Journal*, with the permission of Doubleday & Company, Inc.

Dolphin Books
Doubleday & Company, Inc.

ISBN: *0-385-13472-x*

Copyright © 1978 by Bill Hayward

For Kay

ACKNOWLEDGMENTS

Special thanks to Phyllis Levy for being the best friend a cat or I could have.

To Mike Levins for his excellent prints and steady encouragement and Lindy Hess for her editorial assistance.

INTRODUCTION BY ROGERS E. M. WHITAKER — THE OLD CURMUDGEON

Some of my best friends are cats. Because of my friendship with them, I have been admitted to an international society of immense proportions —Burmese, Maltese, Chinese, Siamese, Senegalese, Abyssinian, Egyptian, Angora, Persian, even Manx; Manx, indeed, those marvelously conceived creations whose forelegs support a face with a Cheshire grin and whose much longer hind legs support a tail that is no more than a rudimentary stump. Manx cats are, I must confess, my favorite slope-up comedians.

Cats represent a civilization far older than any of the several in which I have found myself imbedded from time to time—a civilization at once so simple and yet so subtle that we can never hope to understand it; we must, instead, simply admire. All cats are royalty, or the descendants of royalty; their laws are immutable, and if we civilians are fully to enjoy the pleasures of their company, we, too, must obey their tenets. The advent of later civilizations has had but minuscule effect upon the cat world: a Persian feline never considers himself to be an Iranian; a Siamese cat never deems himself to be a Thailander. These civilizations have, it is true, imposed by main force their will upon the cat world; many a royal scion has by us been torn from family, friends, and throne and compelled to live out his life in exile under an alien sky; cats have even been denied their most precious perquisite—the right to assert their outdoor territorial imperative against all comers—and incarcerated indoors, in city flats, until the end of their days. But a king is forever a king; Napoleon upon Elba was not more imperious toward his staff and his guardians than is a Persian cat suddenly deposited in a milieu wholly foreign to him and no less insistent that, though he be living in exile, his royal prerogatives should be granted him. Nor will mere possession of his earthly body by his captor guarantee possession of the proud creature's soul. Bereft of all familiar landscapes, of all kith, of all kin, a cat may (it is true) enter into an identity crisis, and those in whose pre-

Rogers E. M. Whitaker in his favorite metroline club car with his cat, Torpedo.

cincts he is now to make his new home must prepare themselves to deal properly with the situation. The business of cat nomenclature is not to be undertaken offhandedly. None of us can know of a received cat what name he was given in his faraway royal crib, and his second name —the one we bestow upon him—must be one that the cat can relate to: something having to do, say, with the day he was born, with an oddity of coloration, with a salient idiosyncracy. A Persian born into my own household upon an important moment in the ecclesiastic calendar was christened—sufficient unto the day in question—Epiphany; an up-to-that-point unnamed Angora who came to live with me found such enormous delight in prowling the decks of a municipal ferryboat upon the occasion of his very first outing that he thenceforth bore the name of the vessel in which he was journeying—Edward W. Riegelman. A dappled creature acquired by barter came unnamed under my roof and remained so while I studied with amusement the seven irregular streaks of a pale red that adorned his flanks—remained so until the Widener horse Rosemont won a stakes race at Belmont. An incredibly lanky Siamese, who has but lately entered into my way of life, proceeded, upon his arrival in my premises, to case the joint with such fleetness of foot that Torpedo came instantly to mind.

Never quite fulfilled is the household without a cat or so. The companionship a Persian affords is a foregone conclusion, and a pleasing one; the unquellable curiosity one learns to forgive. For a workingman like me, a cat is the perfect counterpart. After breakfast, and a brief workout to keep down his weight, he is ready for a nap at the very moment I am ready to bend to my daily task. So long as I do not rustle the papers upon my desk too ardently, or ply my electric typewriter with too fierce a fury, he is content to remain asleep, and largely invisible, until the dinner hour. He shares with me my greatest displeasures— sharp and rude noises, prolonged telephone conversations, nearly everything upon the television screen. His curiosity is another matter. Should the laundress deposit a cache of freshly ironed shirts upon the topmost shelf of a closet, he must as speedily as possible determine whether this is the best site for his next dream sequence. His arrival at his destination is announced to me by the thunder of a tumbling tie rack and a brace of traveling cases as he makes his aerial ascent. Then, should I intersperse the row of Christmas cards along the fireplace mantelpiece with a set of drinking glasses that has just descended the holiday chimney, he can thread his way along the precipice without moving a single card as he dissolves all the glassware into shards on the tiling below. But these are merely minor minuses in an otherwise blissful co-existence. Upon occasion, after dinner, he and I have a hand of double solitaire, I dealing and placing the cards, he pointing out with a peremptory paw the errors I appear to have made. And once, when in the evening I was again at my electric typewriter, he was at my elbow (sometimes, it seemed to me, simultaneously at *both* elbows) to riffle through the completed pages and to discard as he saw fit. The interior purring of the machine clearly entranced him; he was puzzled, too, I must assume (as well as I can), about what sort of cheery genie is imprisoned within. It was then explained, in choicest sign language, to I, Claudius, why he must never put his paws inside the contraption, upon pain of electrocution; I myself do not put *my* paws inside, either. There are secrets that it is given neither to man nor to cat to know. Nevertheless, serene in the knowledge that we had effected an interracial understanding, cat and I smiled at each other, and so to bed.

CAT PEOPLE

MOLLY SIPLE

ART DIRECTOR

Lulu

I think it's fascinating how you choose a name for a cat because they kind of have one and you have to discover it. For instance, she was Juliet for several weeks and then somehow Lulu came out. Now it fits perfectly.

I think in their former lives all cats must have been inspectors and proprietors because they're unbelievable fuss-budgets. Like an old French concierge, a cat will really housekeep and see that everything is in order.

I think that cats are great indicators of vibes and personalities and they bring out a lot about people. For example, it might be interesting to have a cat around if you were interviewing someone for a job—you can't fool a cat.

EPHRAIM LONDON

LAWYER

George and Martha

Washington was one of the people whom I always admired a great deal.

Cats are always interesting to watch and be with. Cat movement—I can't think of any other animal that moves as beautifully as a cat.

People who say that cats are not affectionate? I would have two very disappointed cats if I were to ignore them at bedtime. Martha always returns affection by licking you.

MELANIE SCHNEIDER

TV AND RADIO PRODUCER

Siva and Vishnu

They can open all of the doors, drawers, and closets in the house. I will be sitting in the living room with company and suddenly underwear—socks, bras, panties, everything—will just arrive in the living room. I also have to hide the telephone under the sofa if I'm not around. They will answer the phone and leave it off the hook. When I am eating at the table, the cats will go into the kitchen cabinet and bring me the entire box of napkins.

They are much more fun in twos.

PAUL MOORE

EPISCOPAL BISHOP OF NEW YORK

Poochai

Cats are mysterious beings . . . symbols of evil, gods of the Pharaohs. You never know if they love you or if they condescend to occupy your house. This mystery is what makes them the most attractive beast.

SHELLY SMITH

MODEL

Max and Greta

I think that by having a cat you have to be a little more together about yourself. They are sensitive to me, but they are also independent. The other thing that I adore about cats is that they love pleasure; you can just touch them and make them so happy. Sometimes it makes you wish that people you knew could be as warm as that.

JANE PAULEY

TODAY SHOW CO-HOST

Meat Ball

Cat people can be so selfless; it takes quite a person to love a cat who does not obviously adore you. While there are some cats who will jump up and kiss you when you come in, there are other cats who won't give you the time of day unless it's the dinner hour. A cat person will love that cat just as much and maybe a little bit more.

I have found that when you are all wound up, the best tranquilizer in the world is to get one of your cats and stroke it for twenty minutes. It drains everything out of you. If I can't sleep, I just find a cat and stroke it for twenty minutes and all is well. You can't look at a sleeping cat and be tense.

SAMMY BAYES

CHOREOGRAPHER/DIRECTOR

Samson

Vital Statistics:

AGE: 6 years

NATIONALITY: Naturalized American Felidae

PLACE OF BIRTH: Clifton Pub; London, England

SEX: Male

WEIGHT: 13 pounds

MEASUREMENTS: 13″ high × 18″ long

DAILY DRESS: Formal: black tie, spats, etc.

HOBBIES: Swimming; inverted double-palm riding; inverted forearm riding.*

* *Being held upside down and away from one's body on either the hand and forearm, or resting on two inverted palms.*

ROBERTA FLACK

SINGER

Caruso

I think that cat people are very open in their affections. They can give a lot more affection without expecting any open display in return. And, they are a lot more laid back in terms of their environmental surroundings; the home situation is usually very comfortable.

Caruso is very relaxing for me. When I come in, in the morning after a long session, I know he'll meet me at the door. He'll do a little love stretch . . . kind of dance. When cats love you, they stretch for you.

NORA GARDNER

ASSISTANT ART DIRECTOR

Strider

A cat is very self-contained. I like them because they're just more independent and I like when we can get into one another.

Strider really communicates with his tail; when he wants something he will bat you with his tail, but you can't touch it.

Sometimes I think Strider pictures himself as a model. He is beautiful and aloof but not at all pompous. But truth to tell, he's very well-balanced and nonneurotic.

JIM McCANN

INVESTMENT BANKER

Emma, and Kung Tsu (Chinese for Confucius) Sue (Nickname)

Emma likes to take little trips when you're not watching; the ledge goes around the building and so does she. She will visit the woman next door very early in the morning.

Emma loves to go in the water. My mother who is not entirely appreciative of cats was staying here about three weeks ago and she was drawing a bath and all of a sudden I hear this scream. Emma had jumped on the edge of the bathtub and had slid down into the water; Mother didn't take that one very well at all.

One time I had a locksmith here to fix my locks and the locksmith said that he thought that Emma was unattractive, and odd-looking, something like that, and she got so annoyed. She got flat down, pulled her ears back and snarled, and started to stalk him; she kept going toward him and backed him up against the front door and Tzu started bringing up the rear. She gave him a huge snarl and he asked me to stop them, to which I responded that he had insulted her and had to apologize; he then announced that I was crazy. I pointed out to him that you simply cannot go around insulting cats.

LOUISE NEVELSON AND DIANA MacKOWN

ARTIST AND WRITER

Raggedy Ann

My cats will jump on things and run around, but they have never destroyed or touched any of the sculpture. They'll do things to furniture, but they'll never touch the sculpture. There are any number of pieces around here they could climb on, and they won't even get on a piece to inspect it. I think that there are certain awarenesses, vibrations, that go into art that cats might pick up—they might cue into that.

Isn't it possible that there is the same understanding that makes certain animals come to us—cats suddenly showing up—and they know they're meant to be with you?

GENNARO LOMBARDI

RESTAURATEUR

Tiger

Tiger sits out in front of the restaurant every morning, and dozens and dozens of people on their way to work stop and say hello to him and give him a pat on the head. The staff all love Tiger; last night we couldn't find him and we had the chefs and four waiters out in the neighborhood looking for him.

I think that the fascination with cats is that you're constantly working at communicating with them and trying to make them accept you. When do you really win them over? When can I convince this guy that he can trust me and depend on me? I mean, cats decided to domesticate themselves; we have not really domesticated them.

EILEEN FORD

VICE-PRESIDENT OF FORD MODEL AGENCY

Kiki

I really don't know of anything bright to say about cats because I'm so insane for them . . . especially the all-American alley cat. They're street smart and people wise.

Kiki is my most affectionate, lovable friend. The best thing about her is that I can tell her anything and she won't tell a soul; I can count on her to be my confidante.

Cat people—we're just a breed, with great sensitivity and good taste.

J. C. SUARES

GRAPHIC DESIGNER

Maurice, Who, and (No Name)

I'm Egyptian and was brought up in Egypt and I was never allowed to have cats and I was also never allowed to drive, so when I finally came to the United States and moved into an apartment I got a cat and a Rolls-Royce. And then I started multiplying everything . . . so my record number of cats is thirteen and my record number of Rolls-Royces is nineteen.

To this day I find cats a novelty; I'm still amazed that there are cats around the house.

Maurice is the only cat whom I have given a name to; my first wife had a lover by the name of Maurice, and she didn't think that I knew it. And we were lying in bed one morning, the kittens were in the closet and Maurice, then about five weeks old, came out and climbed onto the bed. And my ex-wife said, "Why, you little guy, you're not allowed on the bed." And she grabbed him and said, "What am I gonna call you?" And I said, "Call him Maurice; he's not allowed on the bed either." She put the cat down and she left. So Maurice kept his name.

WANDA TOSCANINI HOROWITZ

CAT PERSON

Bigia

It is very strange that people are still carrying over the fables of the Middle Ages against cats. Cats have been the saviors of this country. At one point in our history, they tried to get rid of cats, and all of the graneries of America were absolutely destroyed by rats. And the story goes that someone brought some more cats in from South America and they became welcome because they saved the crops.

One person who did not used to like cats was my husband; he never liked cats. So until 1966, we never had cats. One night he woke me up and there was a cat hanging around on the terrace making a lot of noise, and he asked me to take him downstairs. Since it was so late, I suggested that we leave him on the terrace . . . and the next morning what do I find but the cat on the foot of my husband's bed? He became the most important person in the house.

I love cats because they are so beautiful aesthetically. They are like sculpture walking around the house.

TERRY FUGATE-WILCOX AND VALERIE SHAKESPEARE

SCULPTOR AND ASSISTANT

Mithra and Bastet

It's very easy to train a cat—just pick anything *they* like to do and tell them to do it.

I was working with steel wool (lots of it) for a sculpture, and I had this one piece laid out, covering about a hundred square feet. I would try different kinds of colors and waters on it to color it, and the cat kept using it for a litter pan. So I put spray on it that is supposed to keep cats away, but that didn't stop him, and I put cayenne pepper in it and that didn't stop him. He just didn't like what I was doing and I haven't worked with steel wool since. It was a pretty honest criticism, I guess, and he was right. It really didn't work out.

CHRIS CRAWFORD

HOMEMAKER

Siegfried

Siegfried will go to any length for attention. On one occasion my husband was interviewing someone here; when I came home, my husband embarrassedly asked me to take Siegfried. He said, "We have not been able to have one bit of conversation. He has eaten the plants, clawed the furniture, climbed up the fireplace" [which he had never done], "and he has brought us papers." He will do the same thing if you are talking on the telephone for too long; his entire life is centered around getting attention. Fortunately, you don't have to call the telephone company to get new telephone cords these days.

To get us up in the morning, he will start chewing on the plants, then the pulls for the curtains, then he goes to the light cord near the bed, then the television antenna, and if that doesn't work, he gets on the desk and pushes things off . . . and this is all within a matter of ten minutes.

DAN GREENBURG

WRITER

Bernie, Ollie, and Maurice

Cats are dangerous companions for writers because cat watching is a near-perfect method of writing avoidance.

Cats are not people. It's important to stress that, because excessive cat watching often leads to the delusion that cats *are* people. For example, it sometimes occurs to me that Maurice is a red-haired Irish newspaper-man-poet who hangs out at bars like the Lion's Head and gets into brawls, and it additionally occurs to me that Ollie is a male model who is very big on Seventh Avenue. Bernie, of course, is a talent agent at William Morris and manages both of their careers.

There is, incidentally, no way of talking about cats that enables one to come off as a sane person.

LAURIE BAKER

METAL SCULPTOR

Wilson

I don't trust people who don't like cats.

When people say they don't like cats because they're too independent, it definitely tells you something about that person. You know that they're not the same kind of person you are.

It amazes me how much pride a cat has. I had a cat who wouldn't be openly affectionate and jump up on your lap; he would come over and sit by you and wait for you to pick him up. They're very sensitive to anything you do.

EMILY COBB

ACTRESS

Scarlet

In the first pictures that my mother ever took of me, there's a cat in my bassinet. I've never been without them.

I had three cats with me at that time and I thought that one didn't have a great deal of talent. His name was Tigger. He was straight out of the Bronx and he was not housebroken. One night I was in *Death of a Salesman* and I went out onto the stage to make up Willie Loman's bed, and I looked and said, "My God, what's in the bed? . . ." It was Tigger and after that there was no getting him off the stage. He succeeded in having the most tremendous career; he ended up being in the *Diary of Anne Frank;* the New York *Times* had "Tiger Cat" signed for the big role and by the following summer he was playing in *Bell, Book, and Candle,* and playing two different productions for *Anne Frank,* and touring the country. He was really in demand, more than I, and making equity minimum: $145 a week.

MARK SEPHTON

FREELANCE MAKE-UP AND HAIRSTYLES
FOR FASHION PHOTOGRAPHY

Charlie

I just like cats for what they are and the way that they look, and I can never see myself without them. They are a constant source of amusement and enjoyment.

A cat is truly everyone's friend. One of the most unusual things that has ever happened is one time a friend of ours left her cat with us for a short while, and when she brought the cat over to the apartment the cat ran outside and hid under the deck for three days. She just wouldn't come out. Finally Charlie, who just loves everyone, went out there and sat under the deck with her for the following two days, until my friend came back and picked up the cat. The poor cat was so hysterical and lonely sitting out there that Charlie took pity on her and he went out and kept her company.

DR. PAUL ROWAN AND CAROL WILBOURN

CAT VETERINARIAN AND CAT BEHAVIORIST

Baggins and Sambo

People who really prefer relating to cats are people who seem to be a good deal more self-aware.

Cats don't think, they feel . . . and that's really what they are all about. Cats are very aware of their bodies . . . as a functioning unit. They always take care of themselves. And that is why it's nice living with them.

When cats were a god image for the Egyptians, it really was because what they were looking for was a whole sense of self-awareness. It was a time when the training of people in that culture was to strive toward a total awareness of all their powers as a person. Because cats were so good at it, they served as models. When cats feel good, they give you so much more; they add a whole dimension to your life. . . .

I guess the way we feel about cats is evident in what we do—we live and work with them all day, every day.

BETSY VON FURSTENBERG

ACTRESS AND WRITER

Minou

I have never had to say no to Minou more than once about anything; it's incredible how much she remembers.

I have always had the feeling that Minou was a reincarnation of a very successful opera star because I would play all kinds of music and, whenever I had opera on, she would go and line her kittens up on the bed, and they would listen to the entire thing from beginning to end, nobody would move until it was over.

Trying to pimp for your cat in New York is really unbelievable. All the males are fixed. I was on the phone for hours trying to find Minou a mate.

I finally managed an arranged marriage with a male cat that belongs to friends. The male cat lived with a female cat and had never shown any interest in her until one evening the male cat was sitting in a window in the apartment during a party; it was dark out, and someone not seeing the cat in the dark sat on the window sill and accidentally knocked the cat out the window. The cat fell about sixteen floors, broke his leg and was in shock, but was alive, and they took him to the vet and miraculously he survived and healed perfectly. When they brought him home, the first thing he did was to impregnate the female cat that he had ignored for so many years.

EDEN LIPSON

EDITOR, NEW YORK TIMES

Cleo

Cats share your most complex intellectual experiences. They stay with me if I am doing handwork, or if I am reading or talking.

A few years ago my apartment was burglarized. The burglar came through the window and thoughtfully closed the cats in the closet so they wouldn't fall out the open window when he left.

ELEANOR AND KEN RAWSON

PUBLISHERS

Sooty

I love to look at cats like I like to look at dancers. A cat is just such an exquisite thing to watch; you see one small cat suddenly turn into something very long, stand on the floor and leap straight up onto something very high with seemingly little effort. There is always a new facet.

During the war I had command of an ammunition ship out in the Pacific, and at some remote port a cat wandered on board the ship and everytime we would go into a port the sailors would watch to see if the cat was going to leave the ship. They were convinced that if the cat ever left the ship it was going to blow up. I said, If that cat ever leaves, I'll have no crew. Fortunately she never left. Everytime we came into port, there was always a group of sailors at the gangway waiting to see if she was going to leave.

I wouldn't say that they are really domesticated. . . . They live with people but they're not dependent on people. They choose to live with people. They don't have to.

MARY ANN MADDEN

NEW YORK MAGAZINE EDITOR

Grace (her tail's name is Doris)

This is the best I was able to do on short notice, what with not being able to get a cat costume and all.

I met Grace in the park nine years ago. I was bicycling and I saw this kitty walking along and I thought she was really cute and she was clearly hungry. I couldn't make the logistics of the bicycle and the cat work, so I came home with the bike and went back for the cat who, of course, had disappeared by then. The next morning, I woke up about six o'clock to turn the air conditioner down because my room was too cold and I heard some people laughing and talking outside. I leaned out the window and there were three young boys about fourteen years old with the cat that I had seen and tried to rescue the day before. I screamed to ask if they found that cat in the park? They said Yes—and I said, It's mine.

Cats are totally captivating because they are so unboring.

KENNY KNEITEL

ART DIRECTOR

Dorothy

The habits that Dorothy and I share are very comfortable. Like every time I come home, before I get the key in the door, I hear this loud thump . . . and it's because she's been sleeping in the loft bed. She hears me come up the stairs and jumps down just when I am getting to the door.

The primary thing about a cat is the aesthetics of the animal. Cats are like very plastic sculptures. Wherever they place themselves, they make an arrangement out of the area that they're in. Whatever they do, they always enhance the area in which they are doing it.

54

NANCY SEAVER

HOMEMAKER

Ferguson

Ferguson is a total baseball cat; he's even named after Ferguson Jenkins, the pitcher.

Every year he goes with us to spring training; he loves Florida where life is one big sandbox.

DRUCIE, MATTHEW, AND THEO SAAL

STUDENTS

Barney and Pippin

Two cats are better than one, and twin cats are even better. Barney and Pippin do everything together; they play together; they sleep together; they explore and get lost together; they clean each other; they follow each other from room to room. They race each other to the top of the scratching post and then knock each other off. They are really so much a part of each other. . . . They go together like peanut butter and jelly.

NOEL BEHN

AUTHOR

(No Name)

I've had two cats each by several girl friends, and the last one was smart enough to leave them here.

Because of the isolation which writers go through, cats are marvelous to have around. I went through weeks on end on this book when I never left this place, and the cat was my only contact with something real. The cat is very much a part of my routine when I write.

The other cat that I had would do a funny thing. When I finished writing for the day, I would put my pages in one place on the desk and he would go through them. He would only go through the pages that I had typed that day and, let's say that I had typed fifteen or twenty pages, about seven or eight of the pages would have teeth marks on them, and I could never tell if he was saying those are the ones to keep or if those are the ones to get rid of.

ANNIE DAMAZ

ART CONSULTANT IN ARCHITECTURE

Matou

Mouche loves melon and prosciutto . . . and he eats them separately but from the same plate. Matou (our other cat) couldn't care less; he is a good American cat who eats canned food.

Cats have a great sense of space and protection, the combination of which is a house.

BEPPE ZAMBONINI

INTERIOR DESIGNER AND EDUCATOR

Cookie

A cat always has design integrity. The way they wash themselves, the way they sit—I cannot think of a cat that's sloppy. Even a street cat, an alley cat, has an elegance that you don't find in any other animal. A very plain common cat can be very beautiful. This cat's mother came from a paint can in the basement of a building and she was absolutely marvel-ous.

I am from Verona, and in Italy, cats are part of the landscape. In all of the Roman and Medieval towns the cat has always been a part of the environment. Cats are part of the culture in Italy.

Holding a cat is a very pleasant experience. . . .

PHYLLIS LEVY

EDITOR

Barnaby and Tulip

There is something about a cat in a house that makes it home. Also a great sense of peacefulness about a cat—a shared peacefulness—a lovely feeling. I love sitting on my bed reading a manuscript with my cats beside me.

A cat is a creature of habit who always wants everything to be in its place and unchanged. You think you know him, but there will always be a little corner of your cat's mind that remains a complete mystery, and so he will always surprise you. That little bit of mystery is wonderful.

The only problem about being a cat person is trying not to turn into a cat freak and bring home every cat who needs you. There are always cats out there who need someone to love them, and cat people love all cats—not just their own.

GEORGE BOOTH

CARTOONIST

Gerbones, Savor-Tooth, and Groucho or Dr. Hackenpuss or Charlie Chaplin

I draw this house all the time, all of the stuff that we have around—the floors, the windows, the ferns, the plants, the chairs, the rugs. I've drawn just about everything that hangs around here . . . so cats were part of the furnishings.

I guess what started me drawing animals is the fact that they are like people; animals do things that I see people do.

I guess Gerbones must be an inspiration to me. In *The New Yorker* cartoon that I repeat of the guy in the bathtub, I have a lot of cats in there and they all look like they are related—well, they are all related to Gerbones. I fell for Dr. Hackenpuss because he looks more like my drawing than the drawings; he's bony, and when he lies down, his back feet go out in back—straight out.

I project people characters into animals: when I'm drawing I get to thinking what the cat is thinking. If you're drawing a nervous cat, for instance, you think about some of the problems that he has—what makes him nervous? Like Gerbones, he's nervous and insecure; he has wrinkles under his eyes and around his brow. . . . He's always worried that he has had his last meal.

GWEN VERDON

ACTRESS-DANCER

Daisy (Super Cat, Fatrick, Feets Fosse, Junie Moon, and Tidbits Tumbler Fosse are playing elsewhere.)

I find that all of the things my cats like to do are the same things I like. I keep getting this feeling that they represent different parts of me, sometimes I'm outgoing and friendly like Fatrick; I enjoy guys just like Daisy; I love basketball as much as Soupy; and I love to fly around just like Tidbits does. Sometimes I'm a loner just like Soupy, who hides under the bed all of the time.

MICHAELE VOLLBRACHT

DESIGNER

Ruth, Mister Skeege, and Mister Botz

Cats have really changed my life immensely and I would never have thought that they would. There is something about watching the interplay of the three of them, it's fabulous. Cats are always doing something; their movements are incredible. They are so predictable in some ways and yet completely unpredictable in others.

People who like cats treat you differently if they know you like cats too —you're okay.

ABBY SCHAEFER

EDITORIAL ASSISTANT

KIRK SIMON

PHOTOGRAPHER, FILMMAKER

Jason and Gazelle

What is amazing about living with cats is that they really seem to know when their form is beautiful; they are very aware of their physicality, of how they are looking. Gazelle, for instance, used to be a good street cat, but now she sits majestically because of being around Jason, who grew up with some very sophisticated cats.

The wonderful uniqueness of a cat is that he can be his own independent being and still be able to love you.

GAIL BENEDICT

DANCER

Reesus, Bert, and Piewacket

Reesus was an acrobat when he was young; he could do triple gainers out of trees. You would put him on top of something and he would jump and flip around and around on his way down. He's too fat to do it now, however. He just spends his time talking now.

They're all great buddies and they're like a gang. I come home and the whole place is redecorated. The furniture is moved, the magazines are repiled, and my desk is reorganized—not necessarily messy, just moved around.

ALVA CHIN

MODEL

Samantha

Cats are so sensitive to you it's incredible. When I'm feeling bad, they always come up and rub and kiss me as if to say "Feel better; feel better."

Cats are very spiritual—more so than humans.

ROBERT INDIANA

ARTIST

Peteepeetoo

I've never gone in search of a cat; they always find me—in Colorado, Maine, on the Bowery. Cats are as much a part of my life as painting. After all, a cat and art are only two letters removed. I know they will always be there.

NANCY NICHOLAS

EDITOR

Blur (*The Gray Blur*)

A word of explanation about her name. The Gray Blur is for her color and her brains. Not, as popularly supposed, for her great speed.

What can I say to tie together being identified as editor with my real vocation as Cat Mother? Our first meeting was like an adorable short story, or really more of a movie. An old cat had died and I went to the cat hospital to get a new kitten. The adoption room is full of cages from the floor to about seven feet up and the people walk around looking at all the orphans and picking the one they want. Suddenly, in mid-stroll, I was stopped by a little gray paw entwined in my hair. That clearly was that.

Her one trick is really not a good one. When I walk in the door, she barks like Lassie in the old movie to tell me the little crippled boy has tipped over his wheelchair and the flames are licking at him and she will lead me to the scene of the tragedy. I follow her, and we always end up in the bathroom; of course there's never anything there. But she has a very proud look, so I always tell her that she has been wonderfully brave.

The only other thing that she does is that she speaks perfect, unaccented French . . . except when strangers are around.

If I lie down to read she comes and sits between me and the book. I think cats are basically anti-intellectual; they want to be between you and the printed word.

In fact, the only reason I agreed to this is that I can show her the picture proudly and know she won't be able to read what I have said about her.

KEN LAX

PHOTOGRAPHER

Muffin

This is Muffin. (Sand, who is just off to the right, weighs ninety-five pounds and has five-inch claws and a brown spot on his nose; he is, in fact, the largest cat in captivity and sets all guidelines for household activities.)

ELLEN SCHECTER

WRITER

Salmagundi

Two years ago I went out to visit some people in the country and on the way we stopped at a vegetable stand. While we were looking around, I saw this lovely Calico cat and I asked the two girls at the stand if they had any kittens. They took me around to a barn and there in a big wicker basket were a series of pint strawberry baskets and in each basket was a kitten . . . one of whom was Salmagundi.

Cats are very symbolic for me. I can tell a lot about people and the way they will treat others by the way that they treat Salmagundi. If someone is particularly one way or the other, and I haven't picked up on it, I very often see it clearly through the way they treat Salmagundi.

I don't brush Salmagundi; she can't stand having the brush forced on her. I hold the brush out and she walks back and forth underneath it . . . then she likes it.

STEWART MOTT

MAVERICK

Morgan

When I have a political fund raiser—unlike most such events when children and pets are not even allowed to be seen or heard—I always allow the cats to wander through. My cats and plants are all around because I enjoy being around living things.

I have had cats in a number of unique living circumstances: a house trailer on a farm in Florida and on a Chinese junk on the Hudson River in New York City. I will always have cats with me no matter where I am. They fit into any environment.

L I Z   S M I T H

D A I L Y   N E W S   C O L U M N I S T

Suzanne and Mr. Ships

Suzanne is a Burmese and she is really my baby, fifteen years of it. Everybody calls her "Zannie"; she's very cuddly and sympathetic but terribly mean to other cats.

Mr. Ships is a street cat who was born on the weekend of the tall ships. He has the legs for it, too. A real domestic shorthair or alley cat. He doesn't like to be handled, but he is very sweet and handsome with his spotless white-and-gray coat. He was so filthy when he was found crying on Thirty-fourth Street near El Parador that it is hard to imagine he is the same cat now, keeping himself so fine.

I have always loved cats. My first cat was an orange tabby named Juicy Pie. I have loved lots of cats—Liza, a white cat with blue eyes (she was deaf); Dennis Bruce, the king of Siamese; Shaunti Graham, the best cat I ever knew—next to Zannie; and Samgram and The Mole, all Golden Siamese—a very fine breed.

The world is divided for me into two kinds of people—those who have had therapy and those who have not. Those who like cats and those who don't. I am not prejudiced against people who don't like cats, or want to experience therapy, but I do know that they are different from those of us who do.

JOHN COHOE

GRAPHIC DESIGNER

Spike

Spike likes brownies and coffee cake; he loves baked goods.

Spike tends to be like a dog sometimes; he carries big steak bones around in his mouth. He can also be a little aggressive. One day we had a little kitten here with Spike, and Spike resented her being in his territory. The kitten fell off the table and was hanging on by its two paws, and Spike was up on the table stomping on the kitten's paws. Cats are very jealous of their own space.

CAROLYN LEFCOURT

DIRECTOR OF LITERARY AFFAIRS AT PARAMOUNT PICTURES

Pasha and B.C.

One of the things that Pasha loves to do is to sit on the edge of the bath-tub and submerge his tail in water and purr. Then he's annoyed when he takes his tail out because it's all wet.

RICHARD MERKIN

PAINTER

Pinky

I think that one warms up to cats, because you are always dealing with cats in a rather intimate way. You deal with your cat when there is nothing else to do and there isn't anyone else there. Cats creep into the most remote and intimate points of your day.

People think about cats in the most secret, coveted kind of way, and cats realize that they have this terrific leverage.

BILL AND HAZEL HAIRE

FASHION DESIGNERS

Rhett, Heathcliff, Ashley, and Uncle Pitty-Pat

Rhett was kidnaped from Geoffrey Beene's factory where I was work-ing as a freelance designer a few years ago. He was the factory cat and one day I noticed that he did not look too well, so I took him to the vet. When I brought him back to the factory, I had trouble finding someone to make sure that he had his medicine every day, so I brought him home and have never returned him. The shipping man was not too happy that I did not bring him back and it was not long after that that I, too, left for good.

BOB TRIANA

PSYCHOTHERAPIST

Csarovitch

I am here about fifteen hours a day, and the thing I became aware of is that everytime I discharged a patient I started feeling somewhat anxious. People were coming and going all the time and I began to feel lonely and isolated. Then I got the cats. Having them around is very reassuring. The patients say that since I have gotten the cats they feel more like they are coming into a home—they feel warmer. There is something that the cats give off in the office that wasn't here before I got them. The cats really reach out to people who come in here . . . someone who's really sobbing. The cat will pick it up and go in their lap.

A lot of my patients are separated, unattached, and they have a sense of isolation, where they just don't feel anything towards anybody. Sometimes I suggest they get a cat, and it's amazing what it's done. The cats have allowed these patients to express warmth for the first time. Some people, before they can even get involved with other people, need animals.

I mean, there are just some things that you can't do for a person that animals can do. . . . Some people can be more expressive to cats because they don't hurt. Other people like cats because they appreciate their feline sense of independence, and they don't feel overwhelmed, controlled, or manipulated by their cats.

HELEN GURLEY BROWN

PUBLISHER COSMOPOLITAN MAGAZINE

Samantha

Unlike most other animals, a cat is ubiquitous. It can be with you all the time, and you can grow to be very close. Cats are very easy to spend time with because they're so unobtrusive; they seem to fit into everything.

Either a cat feels an affinity for you, or it doesn't. This cat really loves me; I am a love object for her and she for me. We're really a disgrace.

LUIS FRANGELLA

ARTIST

Cuco

Observe closely the two pair of eyes—one human, the other animal. The more I live with Cuco, the more I understand what it means to be half animal and half spirit. We are imperfect animals—imperfect, extra-terrestial beings. Just try to communicate a very simple, reasonable fact to a cat. Say for instance: "Please, Cuco, stay quiet because I am doing a delicate water color and need concentration." The cat at this moment could be either staring at me or playing with an empty package of ciga-rettes as if it were a mouse. But, in either case, I have been unable to communicate to the cat. We can only communicate on a primitive level by making little noises to call them for food or hitting them when they use the rolled drawings as a bathroom. Well, it is frustrating to be only half animal, poorly adapted to earth, longing for a world beyond. While cats are better animals than we are, perhaps among the animals, they are the wild ones, because they associate with humans while others, mice for instance, do not want anything to do with us. Mice are proba-bly less corrupted as animals. Or more pure beings. So maybe tigers.

BARBARA LEDERBERG

ADVERTISING EXECUTIVE

Frizbee

She got the name Frizbee because when she was young she would be running through a room and suddenly jump up and off the wall . . . six feet into the air, hit the wall and change direction at the same time and be off somewhere else.

She's very much a part of the family and her comfort is very high on our list of priorities. Unfortunately she's not very sophisticated in her choice of food. She only eats a little boiled ham from time to time, and you really have to force whipped cream down her throat. She only eats cat food, so she's really a pain. I've tried lobster, or I've tried crab; I've even tried shrimp, both raw and cooked, and . . . nothing. I don't know where she gets her taste from.

She has to have an electric blanket; she won't go to sleep unless the electric blanket is on. As soon as you turn it on, she's on it. If she ever had to leave, we'd have to give her a long extension cord for her blanket.

She does come when you call . . . but only after you've given up.

DICK SCHAAP AND DAUGHTER JOANNA A. SCHAAP

AUTHOR/JOURNALIST

Ghandi

My cat originally belonged to my elocution teacher. Later, it occurred to me it would be cheaper to take diction lessons from the cat, since he sat in on so many lessons. And as a bonus, I found out I can get the cat to do my legwork. For instance, he often goes over to interview Tom Seaver's cat and pads back with reams of information. Every journalist should have a cat.

LOUISE SARACINO

CANDY STORE LADY

Lady

You've heard of night people and cat people; I'm a cat people.

I say to everyone . . . Get a cat! It's a cat that's a man's best friend.

SUSIE FRANKFURT

INTERIOR DESIGNER

Sammy

I think that I look like my cat.

The cat knows that he's a great visual. The cat instinctively has great style; he knows where to put it and where to go with it. He's really color-co-ordinated. He knows he looks good with beige.

He loves to sit near anything new and expensive; any time I get something new in the house, that becomes his seat until we get something else that's newer—and more expensive. I've got a house full of beautiful objects, but I like the cat best of all. He's better than all of the Buddhas I have sitting around. He's alive.

A cat is eternal—a real stoic; he looks like he's been around for three thousand years. He must have lived in Persepolis at some time or Egypt. The look of my cat is historic and hysteric.

DR. LOUIS CAMUTI

CAT VETERINARIAN

I started specializing in just cats about 1932–33—vets weren't spending much time on cats in those days—but the cat was always a big thing with me in my life, because I always felt that maybe it saved my life a long time back. When I was about eleven years old I had typhoid fever, and in those days they treated typhoid by putting you in bed and keeping you in bed with no food. Only a little liquid now and then. Now they feed you to death, but in those days it was the opposite. My mother had been called by a neighbor who was sick and she left something on the stove and it boiled over and gas fumes came into my room, and this cat of mine jumped up on my chest and kept weaving her head back and forth so I could breathe. I couldn't get out of bed—I was so weak—until my mother came back.

I started making house calls from the very beginning of my work. I had an office, but I always felt that an animal should be treated in its home surroundings. They would never be at their best in an office. When I gave up my last office, because they pulled down the building that I was in, I went to 100 per cent house calls and I was glad to do it . . . sitting in the office was not something I liked.

BILL AND JANE LEWIS

OWNER OF PERSONNEL AGENCY AND EDITORIAL ASSISTANT

Fiss

Fiss was named after a misprint in a Chinese menu—you know, there's "meat," "poultry," and "fiss." Our favorite restaurant at the time was a Chinese restaurant and we had just gotten the cat and didn't know what to name him.

The alternative is now to get rid of the cats or buy a bigger houseboat. Instead of getting rid of the cats, we're buying a bigger boat. Yes, they do fall in the water, especially Fiss. He is this big tomcat and you would think that he could take care of himself.

DOROTHY GALLAGHER

AUTHOR

Emily

I gave her the name Emily because she looked like a picture-postcard kitten. A Victorian blond child.

SALLY JEANCON

CAT PERSON

Willow

Cats definitely have unique personalities. They really know who they are, and they are honest and direct. Willow is very moody, and you can tell by his face what mood he is in.

I definitely have an affinity for people who like cats.

AMANDA VAILL AND TOM STEWART

EDITORS

Sasha and Tania

Sasha is eight and Tania is two—both of them were born near water of a sort, Sasha in a shower in Adams House, an undergraduate dorm at Harvard, and Tania under a boathouse in Northport, Long Island. They really are complete opposites. Sasha is a true paranoid and like all true paranoids she's happiest when the world conforms to her view of it, so she loves loud thunderstorms and big barking dogs and traveling in strange places. Tania is more like a marshmallow—white and soft and sweet—and she's practically afraid of her own shadow. Oddly, Tania usually wins their mock battles, although Sasha screams loudest during them; Tania saves her voice for demanding her breakfast, loudly and shrilly, at 7 A.M. When this doesn't get us up, she starts washing us with her very scratchy tongue, or she knocks things off the dresser, or starts playing with the rubber bands around any manuscripts that might be lying about. She plunks them with her teeth.

We have built up a whole mythology around these cats. For instance, we firmly believe that Sasha learned about the Territorial Imperative (a principle she defends vigorously) from Dan Ardrey, the son of Robert Ardrey, who was one of the three roommates in whose suite she grew up at Harvard. We maintain that she got love of heights—she loves to jump up on the tops of doors and sit there like a gargoyle—from Julian Sorel, the hero of one of her favorite books, *The Red and the Black*. And it was she, we think, who insisted we name the new white kitten Tania in commemoration of the SLA and Patty Hearst. Tania, however, thinks she was named for Titania, the fairy queen; we used to be certain that she was a foolish princess who had been turned by magic into a milk-white cat with one blue eye and one brown eye and an abnormally long tail, which, for some reason, she loves to have pulled. We're not sure why she was turned into a cat, unless it was to make it easier for her to crawl under sofas and behind sinks or stoves and into narrow dirty places where she can get absolutely filthy—which is her favorite thing to be.

ANITA SUMMER

COLUMNIST

Tibby

I love cats.

The day our new bathroom was being installed the workmen were coming in and out, so I sat in the kitchen with Tibby to watch her. The telephone rang in my office and when I got back to the kitchen, Tibby was gone. I searched the entire house and couldn't find her anywhere; we looked all around the neighborhood and still no luck. At seven that evening we heard a muffled meow. So we rushed around the house to determine where the sound was coming from, and we ended up in the newly finished bathroom. The first meow was from the ceiling so we ripped out most of the ceiling—she wasn't there. Every half-hour we heard another meow coming from a different area and eventually ripped out every piece of sheet rock in the bathroom and still couldn't find her, but we could still hear her meowing. The last meow came from under the bathtub, so we went into the basement and started ripping out some of the ceiling tiles. Finally at one-thirty in the morning we pulled her by the tail into safety. When the workmen came the next day they were absolutely amazed.

KATHRIN SEITZ

EXECUTIVE PRODUCER OF MOVIES AND NOVELS FOR TELEVISION, ABC-TV

Priscilla

She came with the apartment.

DR. JOHN PRUTTING

INTERNIST

Oz

Oz appeared at my back door about six years ago, which is interesting when you consider that I live on the top floor of an apartment building.

Oz is a big football player of a cat, a husky linebacker. He will barge through anything and literally doesn't know when to come in out of the rain. He's the only cat I know who, after he has been given an injection, will graciously walk the vet to the door. He loves everyone.

Cats are so very relaxing and therapeutic. They never, never tire you out; they lie and move so comfortably.

JEAN PAUL GOUDE

ARTIST

Sapphire

Sapphire is from Alabama and she must have had a very heavy childhood down there, because she is the most boring person I know. She is both boring and bored—absolutely nothing interests her. Nothing can get her attention.

I don't get any respect from her; she takes absolutely everything for granted and abuses me all of the time—never a thank-you. In fact, she treats me like a dog. She's this lazy, savvy, beautiful woman with an incredible "attitude." A real hustler.

MR. AND MRS. D. H. TOLLER-BOND

PRESIDENT LONDON RECORDS AND HOMEMAKER

Benjamin

We've been married twenty-nine years and we've always had cats, and I think that's the only reason my husband married me—because I had a cat.

People always think that because they are independent, cats cannot be devoted to you, but they absolutely can be. We've had cats forever.

ELIZABETH HESS

MAGAZINE EDITOR

Piet

I first spied this handsome devil walking out of the Cedar Tavern on University Place. He was scratching his ears, debating whether to prowl on up to the Elgin to catch the Cat Film Festival.

Knowing that few cats in the village are half that svelte (let alone have any interest in feline cinema), I didn't mind when he rubbed against my ankle before introducing himself. In fact, I wasn't even paranoid when he followed me home. (Been with Piet ever since.)

We don't go to the movies much these days because there's cat violence in every film—during Bertolucci's *1900* we broke all our nails.

Lately we've taken to sitting out on the fire escape munching on Purina, watching the street cats do their hustle. Piet's considering trying out for the new Bakshi film—*The Return of Fritz the Cat*—or maybe starting his own feline film magazine, *The Cat's Meow.*

RICHARD KNAPPLE

HOME-FURNISHINGS FASHION DIRECTOR, BLOOMINGDALE'S

Tunafish

You have to prove yourself to a cat and that can take months. They're incredible at hiding both themselves and their feelings. At first Tunafish would drive me crazy. Here I took this poor thing off the street and gave her a home, lavished her with affection, and I got nothing in return for months. Then, all of a sudden, she trusted me and now she won't leave me alone.

I think cats attract the more sensuous person.

MORT GOTTLIEB

THEATER AND MOVIE PRODUCER

Veronica

Very often I'll read scripts stretched out on the couch, and Veronica will come and lie on my stomach facing the script. I can see her head moving left to right, looking at each line. Eventually, her head is lowered till it's at the bottom of the page. Sometimes she'll wait for me to turn the page and start again at the top, little by little working her way down. One time, after a few pages of this she turned to me and shook her head. Needless to say, it never got produced.

The most special thing about Veronica?—the fact that she's here.

FONTAYNE

COUTURIER

Sable

I have had cats forever . . . and personally I am totally feline. People who love cats are free and open and easy.

The way that I acquired Sable was marvelous. I had a friend who was a breeder, and she fell in love with a cocktail dress in my collection. I traded her the dress for my pussycat. That cocktail dress was probably discarded some time ago, and sixteen years later he is still the joy of my life.

The accolade that all of my beaus try for is to have Sable jump up in their laps. I was seeing someone for a year and a half, and Sable jumped up in his lap twice and you would have thought that he had won the Nobel Peace Prize. He was so thrilled, he was afraid to move.

Sable sleeps on a saga blue-fox coat.

MARCO GLAVIANO

FASHION PHOTOGRAPHER

YASMINE SOKAL

MODEL

Puff Puff and Bou-Boul

Puff Puff is constantly running around the studio getting into things—like chewing on prints and light cables and backgrounds. He especially loves being photographed. When Marco is shooting, he will get on the background paper and won't move. He has been in Bloomingdale's and *Mademoiselle* ads.

He's always very nice to the models . . . and loves to lick their make-up and hide in their garment bags.

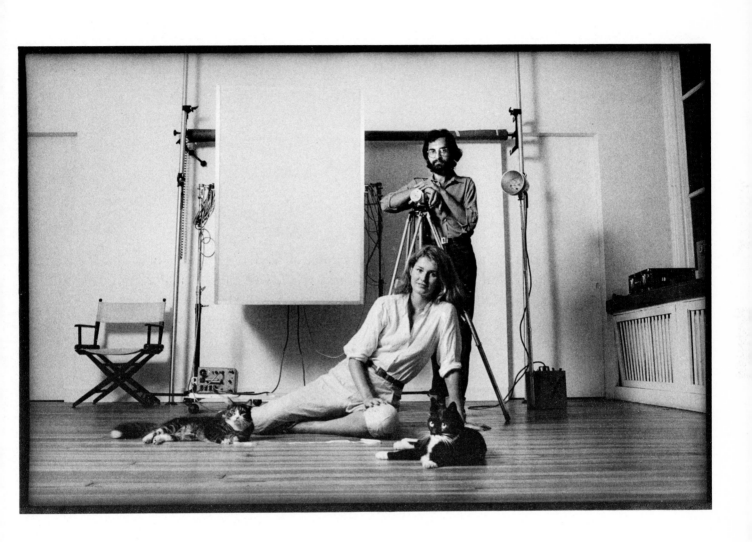

KARL HARTIG

VIDEOPHILE/MECHANICAL ARTIST

Tiny

Cats live in a different world of phenomena, and if you are going to have any kind of relationships with them at all, you have to understand they live by a different set of rules and priorities. (Many of their perceptions are much more developed than ours.) We share the same space with two different patterns of activity coexisting.

MISS ANITRA

CAT GROOMER

Purr, Priscilla, and Florence

I love the milieu of cats and I am grateful for their allowing me in; I live and work with cats.

The thing that is so special about cats is their total honesty; they are incapable of lying. If I am grooming a cat and the cat says stop—I listen; I don't ignore it. Cat etiquette is very important if you want to get along with a cat; there are many things that you've got to know. You never, for instance, pick up a cat without announcing yourself.

If I am meditating, a cat will always come over to me and will go into a steady mind state and enjoy it and drink it with you.

BARRY FARBER

RADIO HOST AND POLITICIAN

Frankie

Watch the cat. Try to find one move, tactic, or caprice that doesn't contain the elegance of professional ballet.

I think God gave us cats to help shed majesty into the lives of people too hurried, insensitive, or dumb to appreciate poetry.

SEYMOUR AND PAULA CHWAST

DESIGNERS

Mary

Getting cats is a greater commitment than getting married.

I like the degree of pride that cats have; they really enjoy being what they are. There seems to be no dissatisfaction in their lives; they're not critical and don't care if the silverware is shined. It's better than having your mother live with you.

The thing that is very satisfying about cats is the way they show their appreciation—the most terrific thing in the world is hearing a cat purr.

RUTH LEVY

TEACHER

Sammy

It's amazing; if I'm out and there is someone in the house, they always know when I'm coming home five minutes or so before I get here, because wherever Sammy is, he can be fast asleep, he suddenly darts for the door and sits there. He is always waiting at the door when I come in. If a cat becomes attached to you, you really feel that you've succeeded.

Sammy's greatest joy is going into people's homes; he likes to visit. Also he loves to sit on his stool and admire himself in the mirror.

BETH RASHBAUM AND FRANK ROSE

EDITOR AND MAGAZINE WRITER

Smoke and Casper

Smoke and Casper are very different cats. Smoke is athletic and somewhat doglike in that he fetches and comes when he is called. He particularly likes to fetch the tabs from cans of frozen orange juice. He could be asleep in the closet, but if you go into the kitchen and open a can of orange juice he will hear you and come bounding in. The solution is to leave Smoke in the kitchen and open the orange juice in the closet.

Casper, on the other hand, is a sissy. He is a shy, langourous creature who leads a very intense and secret life. He will lie on a radiator for hours with his legs and his tail trailing gracefully down to the floor. Casper's destiny is intimately linked with the scent of Jungle Gardenia. He arrived at our door draped over the bosom of his mistress. We thought the perfume was hers, but after she left it took two weeks for the scent to dissipate. He no longer drapes himself over anyone's bosom, but we don't use Jungle Gardenia either. We're not sure how this has affected his personality, but he does tend to whine a lot.

GENE SHALIT

CRITIC FOR NBC-TV AND WRITER

Junior

Photographer's Note:

There are times perhaps when the story value of a photograph may exceed the proverbial thousand-word limit set by the Chinese. For example I feel that this is one "cat story" that is almost revealing in its photographic form—no verbalization could possibly enhance its telling.

A NOTE FROM THE PHOTOGRAPHER

When I originally conceived of this book, there was a period of time when it belonged to me; but the duration of that ownership was short-lived indeed. I had no idea that the book would suddenly gain a terrific momentum of its own, and like a perpetual-motion machine, there was no stopping it.

To be sure, this book really belongs to the people and the cats inside. I was simply a privileged passenger on their train, and what an exciting ride it was. One cat person was always the source of at least three or four other cat people, and complete strangers would suddenly appear as earnest researchers. Cat people and cat stories were everywhere.

Perhaps the most exciting part of these encounters, however, was the experience in human relations. If you really want to know people, ask them about their cats.

People's relationships with their cats tend to be an exotic blend of the emotional and intellectual, based on a complete and total sense of honesty. As so often came up in these interviews: "You have to be totally honest in your relationship with a cat because they are so completely in control of themselves and so honest in all that they do." For this reason, I found Cat People to be uniquely generous, open, and unself-conscious when talking about themselves and their cats, and what a wonderful way to come to know people.

INDEX